AN INTRODUCTION TO LINUX PROGRAMMING

BEGINNER'S GUIDE TO LINUX PROGRAMMING

DAVID LIVINGSTON J

Contents

CHAPTER ONE

Introduction to Linux

n 1969, Thompson and Ritchie designed and built an OS having an elegant file system, a command interpreter (called shell), and a set of utilities. In 1973, they rewrote the entire system in C - a high level programming language that was invented by Ritchie himself.

The University of California, Berkley (UCB) created a UNIX of its own and was named BSD UNIX (Berkley Software Distribution UNIX). These versions became popular worldwide, especially in universities and engineering circles.

Sun used the BSD system as a foundation for developing their own brand of UNIX and named it SunOS. Today, their version of UNIX is known as Sun Solaris. Similarly, there are other flavors of UNIX developed over a period of time: IBM's AIX, HP-UX, DEC's Digital UNIX and Tru64 UNIX. Then the Linux wave arrived and most of these vendors are offering Linux too. Today, most supercomputers run UNIX, and handheld devices are using Linux.

Linux - A Successor of Unix:

Linux was developed having UNIX as a reference model. Therefore, the basic architecture and features of Linux and UNIX are the same. In fact, Linux is also considered as another version of UNIX. The main difference between Linux and UNIX is that Linux is free and open source. However, various distributors of Linux can charge a price for Linux. In addition, Linux doesn't involve any licensing issues.

Linux is licensed under the General Public License (GNU). This licensing policy states that a person can make any number of copies of software and distribute it freely, or charge a price for it. But, the source code must be provided along with the product.

Although, UNIX finally turned commercial, Richard Stallman and Linux Torvalds (father of Linux) wanted to develop and distribute a free version of UNIX. Stallman is the founder of Free Software Foundation, formerly known as GNU - a recursive acronym for "GNU's Not Unix." Many of the important Linux tools were written and supported free by GNU.

Linux is distributed under the GNU General Public License, which makes it mandatory for developers and sellers to make the source code public. The most popular GNU/Linux flavors are: RedHat, Caldera, SuSE, Debian and Mandrake. We can download Linux free of cost from the Internet.

Linux - An Open Source OS:

Linux was developed as a cooperative effort over the Internet, so no company or institution controls Linux. Software developed for Linux reflects this background. Development often takes place when Linux users decide to work on a project together. When completed, the software is posted at an Internet site, and any Linux user can then access the site and download the software.

The potential for Linux-based software is explosive. Linux software development always takes place in an Internet environment and it is global in scope, enlisting programmers from around the world. The only thing we need to start a Linux-based software project is a web site.

Most Linux software is developed as open source software. This means that the source code for an application is freely distributed along with the application. Programmers over the internet can make their own contributions to a software's development, modification and upgradation of the source code.

Linux is particularly strong in networking and cost-effective in setting up an Internet Server or a local internet. Linux has development tools, such as C, C++, FORTRAN, Pascal and scripting languages such as awk, Perl and Python. Many of these scripting languages are free of cost. Moreover, Web Servers (such as Apache) and Web Browsers (such as Netscape) provide their versions that are compatible with Linux, free of cost.

CHAPTER TWO

Evolution of Linux

In 1969, Ken Thompson and Dennis Ritchie developed a small, general-purpose Operating System called UNIX. Traditionally, all operating systems were written in the assembly language and so was UNIX. In 1973, Thompson and Ritchie rewrote the UNIX OS in C. In 1974, UNIX was licensed to universities for educational purposes and made commercially available later.

Many vendors, such as Sun, IBM, and Hewlett-Packard, purchased the source code of UNIX and developed their own version of UNIX. Most of these versions were proprietary and maintained by their respective hardware vendors. The source code of these versions were not freely available, so the developers had to wait for a long time for the release of bug fixes.

In 1984, Richard Stallman's Free Software Foundation (FSF) began the GNU (GNU's Not UNIX) project to create a free version of the UNIX OS. By 1990, the FSF developed a number of tools for an OS like Unix but the kernel was still not created. The software tools developed by FSF were freely available along with the source code for analysis, modification and redistribution.

In 1991, Linus Torvalds developed a kernel and called it Linux. In 1992, the Linux kernel was combined with the incomplete GNU system to form a completely free OS. This OS is called GNU/Linux because it is a combination of GNU and Linux. The GNU/Linux OS is commonly referred to as the Linux OS.

There are several distributors of Linux. All the distributors use the Linux kernel. Some of the distributors of Linux are given below:

Distributor Name	Web Site
Red Hat	http://www.redhat.com
Caldera	http://www.caldera.com
Mandrake	http://www.linux-mandrake.com
Debian	http://www.debian.org
SuSE	http://www.suse.com
Slackware	http://www.slackware.com

The Structure of Linux OS:

Linux follows the open development model. Therefore, the current development version of Linux is always open to users. Users can suggest modifications to the kernel code. When a new version of Linux is released, users can work on the new version to fix bugs, if any.

To maintain stability, Linus Torvalds ensures strict quality control and then merges all the new code into the kernel. This is in contrast to a closed model in which a project team develops a particular software version and waits before users can work on it and report bugs. The project team then fixes the bugs and releases a new version.

Linux has an official mascot – the Linux penguin – called Tux. Moreover, Linux has its own free software tools - text editors, browsers, and programming tools. The GNU/Linux OS consists of a kernel, a shell, utilities and application programs as shown in the below figure:

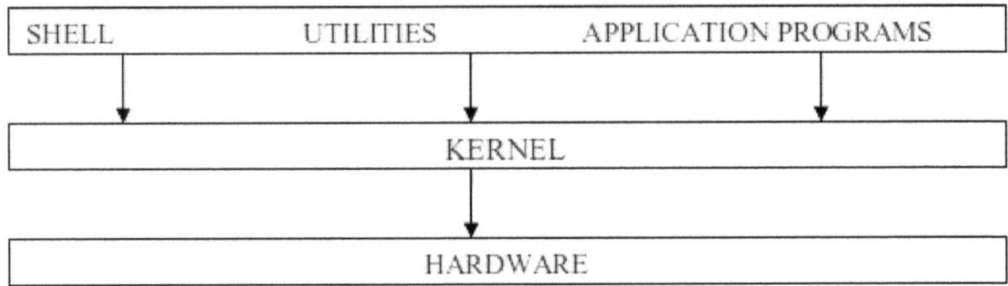

Components of Linux OS

Linux Components - Kernel and Shell:

The core of the Linux system is the **kernel**, which controls the resources of a computer, allocating them to different users and tasks. It interacts directly with the hardware, making programs easy to write and portable across different hardware platforms. However, the user doesn't interact directly with a kernel. Instead, the logon process initiates a separate, interactive program called the shell for each user.

Linux has a simple user interface called **shell**. The shell provides services to its users. Users interact with the computer by using the shell. They need not know about the intricate details of the hardware. Some of the common shells in Linux are **bash**, **sh**, **tcsh**, **csh** and **ksh**.

Linux utilities or commands are a collection of programs that service processing requirements. These programs can be started by using the shell. In addition to the utilities that are part of the Linux OS, many Linux-based application programs, such as Database Management Systems and Word Processors are available from independent vendors.

Features of Linux OS:

Linux is an Operating System for PC computers and workstations that now features a fully functional **Graphical User Interface (GUI)** just like Windows and the MAC OS. Linux is a PC version of the UNIX OS that has been used for decades on mainframes and minicomputers, and is currently the system of choice for workstations.

Linux brings the **speed, efficiently, and flexibility** of UNIX to our PC, taking advantage of all the capabilities those personal computers can now provide. Along with its UNIX capabilities, come powerful **networking** features, including support for Internet, intranets, Windows, and AppleTalk networking. As a standard, Linux is distributed with fast, efficient, and stable Internet servers, such as the Web, FTP and Gopher servers, along with the domain name, proxy, news, mail and indexing servers.

Some of the other features of Linux OS are multiprogramming, time-sharing, multitasking and free licensing. Linux allows several programs to be executed simultaneously by its users. This feature is called **multiprogramming**. Multiprogramming is possible on Linux through time-sharing.

In **time-sharing**, the OS has to manager various programs simultaneously. Programs are queued, and CPU time is shared among programs. Each program receives the CPU time for a specific period and is then replaced in the queue.

Every program is broken down into tasks, such as reading from or writing to the disk or waiting for input from a user. The ability of any OS to handle the execution of multiple tasks is known as **multitasking**. When a task is waiting for the completion of another task, the CPU instead of wasting its time in waiting, starts executing the next task. Therefore, while one task is waiting for input from the user, another task could be reading from the hard disk. This process of scheduling multiple tasks to a single CPU is taken care by the kernel.

CHAPTER THREE

Overview of Linux

Like UNIX, Linux can be generally divided into three major components: the **kernel**, the **environment**, and the **file structure**. The **kernel** is the core component that runs programs and manages hardware devices, such as disks and printers. The **environment** provides an interface for the users. It receives commands from the user and sends those commands to the kernel for execution.

Linux OS Structure

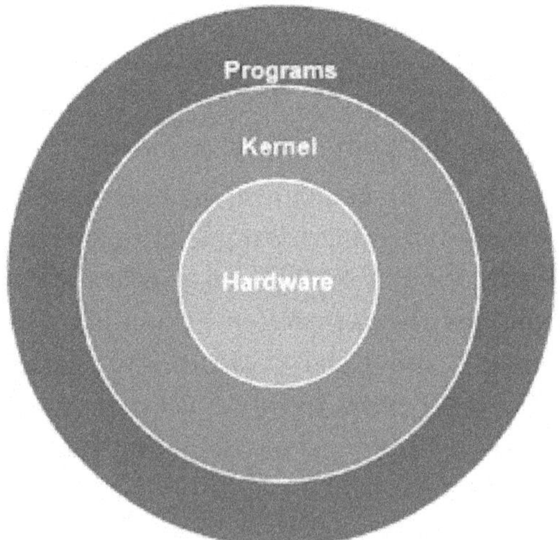

An **environment** acts an interface between the kernel and the user. It can be considered as an interpreter, because it interprets commands entered by the user and sends them to the kernel. Linux provides three **kinds of environments**: desktops, window managers, and command line shells.

The **file structure** organizes the way files are stored on a storage device, such as a disk. Files are organized into directories. Each directory may contain any number of sub directories, each holding files. Together, the kernel, the environment, and the file structure form the basic operating system structure. With these three, we can run programs, manage files, and interact with the system.

Advantages of Linux OS:

Linux is a fully functional UNIX OS. It has all the standard features of a powerful UNIX OS, including a complete set of UNIX shells such as **bash**, **tcsh**, and the **Z shell**. Those familiar with the UNIX interface can use any of these shell, with the same UNIX commands, filters, and configuration features.

For Internet users, Linux has provides a platform for running very powerful Internet applications. With Linux, we can create our own Web, FTP, and Gopher sites. Other users can access our Linux system, several at the same time, using different services.

Using Linux, we can control access, set up network connections, and install new devices. Linux includes very powerful and easy-to-use, window and web-based configuration utilities like **Lunuxconf** and **Webmin**, which can be used to perform system administrative tasks such as installing printers, adding users, and establishing new network connections.

A wide array of applications operate on Linux. Many personal versions of commercial applications such as **WordPerfect** and **Sybase** database are available for Linux free of charge. We can download them directly from the Internet. Moreover, a massive amount of software is available at online Linux sites where we can down them and install them onto a Linux system.

Types of Linux Environment (UI):

Each user on a Linux system can have his (or her) own user interface. Users can tailor their environments to their own special needs, whether they be shells, window managers, or desktops. The shell interface is simple and usually consists of a prompt at which the users type a command, and then press ENTER.

Over the years, several different kinds of shells have been developed and, currently, three major shells exist: **Bourne**, **Korn** and **C shell**. Among these three, the C shell was developed for the BSD version of UNIX.

As an alternative to a command line interface, Linux provides two different versions of GUI - desktop and window manager. A desktop provides a complete GUI, much like Windows and MAC. A window manager, on the other hand, is a reduced version of desktop, supporting only window operation, but it still enables the user to run any application.

In desktop environment, we have desktops, icons, and menus, all managed through mouse controls. Currently, two different desktops are freely available and both are included with most distributions of Linux: **Gnome** and **KDE**. With these two desktops - K Desktop Environment (KDE) and GNU Network Object Model Environment (GNOME), Linux now has a completely integrated GUI interface. We can perform all our Linux operations entirely from either interface.

Features of KDE and GNOME:

KDE and GNOME are fully operational desktops supporting drag-and-drop operations, enabling the user to drag icons to the desktop and to set up menus on an Application panel. Both rely on an underlying X Windows system, which means as long as they (KDE and GNOME) are installed on a system, application from one can run on the other desktop.

We can run KDE programs like KDE mailer or the newsreader on the Gnome desktop. Gnome applications such as Gftp (a FTP client) can run on the KDE desktop. The major difference between these two desktops is that the K desktop has a complete set of Internet tools, along with editors, graphics, multimedia, and system applications, but Gnome has slightly fewer applications.

A great deal of Linux software is currently available from online sources. We can download applications for desktops, Internet servers, Office suites, programming packages, among others. Software packages are distributed either in compressed archives or in RPM packages. RPM packages are those archived using the Red Hat Package Manager. Compressed archives have an extension such as .tar.gz or .tar.z, whereas RPM packages have an .rpm extension.

Samba and Apache:

The name Samba is derived from the Server Message Block protocol or SMB. SMB is the protocol used by Microsoft OS to share files and printers. Samba is a suite of programs that implement the SMB protocol on Linux.

Using Samba, we can share machines running Windows 95, Windows 98 or Windows NT with our Linux machine. Not only files, but also printers managed by Windows OS can be shared with Linux through SMB.

Linux OS comes with a web server named Apache. A Web server enables its users to access resources on a Wide Area Network or the Internet. It is considered as a process that runs on a server and enables users to access resources that have been published in the form of web pages.

For example, when the user enters the address of a web site, say www.apache.org, in a web browser, the Apache Web Server sends the home page of the web site to the client machine. Generally, a Web Server is referred to as a computer that delivers web pages.

CHAPTER FOUR

The Kernel and Shell

Linux is a powerful multi-user Operating System. It provides its basic functionalities through two of its layers namely **Kernel** and **Shell**. Ther Kernel is the inner most part of the OS, and it directly interacts with the machine's hardware. The shell acts as an interface between the user and the kernel, enabling the user to enter commands for the OS to execute.

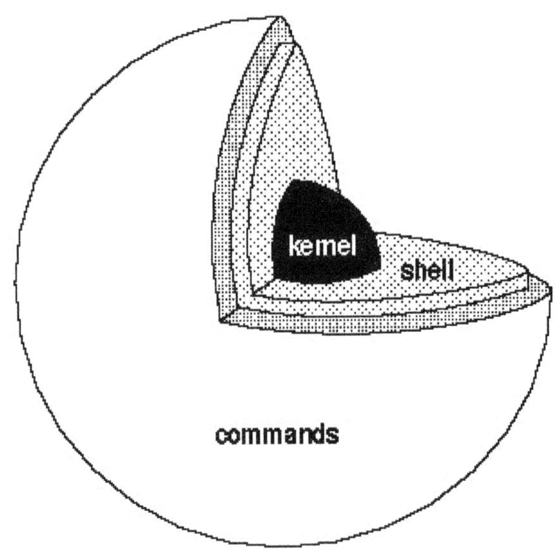

Kernel and Shell of Linux OS

The Kernel is the core part of the OS and is implemented as a collection of routines mostly written in C. Kernel gets loaded into memory when the system is booted. User programs (called applications) that need to access the hardware should make use of the services provided by the kernel through a set of functions called system calls.

Apart from providing support to user programs, the kernel has other responsibilities that include:

1. Managing the system's memory
2. Scheduling processes and
3. Deciding the priority of processes ready for execution

Thus the OS is a system software that acts as a gateway between the user and the hardware resources available on the computer. A user can login to a Linux system by entering a user name assigned by the System Administrator, and a password. And terminate or logout a session by using the exit command or pressing ctrl-d.

The Shell:

UNIX, Linux's inspiration, originally had no graphical interface at all; everything was done from the command line. It resembles the Windows command prompt, but Linux shells are much more powerful than the command prompt of Windows OS.

Shell is a program that constantly runs at the terminal as long as the user is logged in. It has a command interpreter which takes care of translating shell commands into action. Linux users can make use of the shell to enter and execute linux commands.

At the command prompt (called terminal), we can use some special symbols such as *****, <, > and | along with the linux commands. The symbol * can be used to capture a number of filenames with a simple pattern. The symbols < and > can be used to redirect the input and output from standard I/O devices, while | (pipe symbol) feeds the output of one command as the input to another command.

When a user enters a linux command through the keyboard, the shell throughly examines the keyboard input for special characters. If it finds any, it rebuilds a simplified command line, and finally communicates it with the kernel for execution.

On Linux, the standard shell that is always installed as **/bin/sh** is called **bash** (the GNU Bourne-Agaom SHell), from the GNU suite of tools. Bash shell is open-source, and is portable at atmost all UNIX variants. User can check the version of bash with the following command:

$/bin/bash --version

Other shell available either free or commercially are namely **C Shell** (csh) and **Korn Shell** (ksh). Korn shell is an advanced shell from AT&T, which has a unique number 364 as its process-id (PID).

One of these shells will run to serve the user after log in. Linux uses the Bash shell as default, though it offers the C Shell and Korn Shell as well. To knwo the shell that is running currently, we use the command:

echo $SHELL

Files and Processes:

Files and processes are the two basic entities that support the existance of Linux OS. A file is just an array of bytes and contains virtually anything. A file is related to another file by being part of a single hierarchical structure.

Linux has a large number of files that control its functionity. Users can also create files on their own. The **ls** command displays all the filesnames and folders in the current directory. **ls** command can also be used along with an option **-l** (between the command and filenames given as parameter) to know more about the files available in the directory as follows:

$ls -l

A **process** refers to a file being executed as a program. In other words, a process is simply the "time image" of an executable file. We can consider processes as living organism since they are born and die, having parent-child relationship with other processes. All processes running in Linux belong to a separate hierarchical structure.

Every program that we run at the terminal gives rise to a process, and the shell is a process as well. The shell program is always running at the terminal. **ps** command will display all the processes running currently. The following is a sample output generated by **ls** and **ps** commands at the terminal:

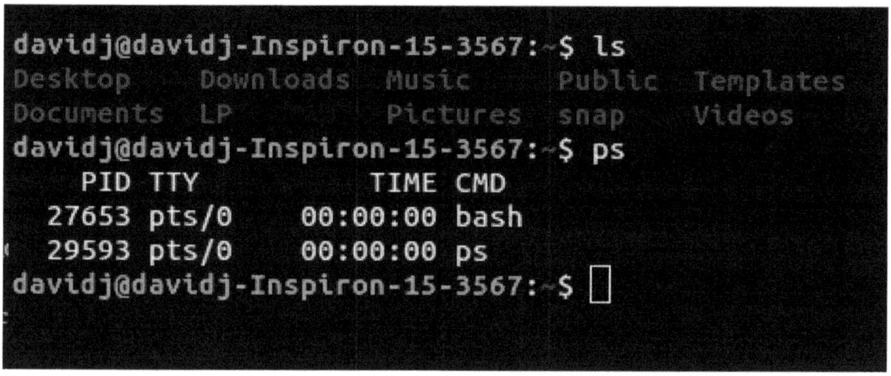

```
davidj@davidj-Inspiron-15-3567:~$ ls
Desktop    Downloads  Music     Public  Templates
Documents  LP         Pictures  snap    Videos
davidj@davidj-Inspiron-15-3567:~$ ps
    PID TTY          TIME CMD
  27653 pts/0    00:00:00 bash
  29593 pts/0    00:00:00 ps
davidj@davidj-Inspiron-15-3567:~$
```

Sample Run of ls and ps Commands

In the output of ps command, we have a header followed by the details of all the processes running currently by the kernel.

Directing Output to a File:

Linux lets the output produced by the ls command to be stored in a file if the user uses a special symbol > (the right chevron character) in the ls command as follows:

$ls > list

This command redirects the output produced by ls command to a file named list. After its execution the prompt returns without displaying anything on the terminal. To check whether the shell has actually done the job, use the **cat** command with the filename as an argument:

$cat list

The cat command when a file name is given as an argument displays the content of that file on the screen. To know more about the file, such as numer of lines, words and characters in a file, we use **wc** command:

$wc list

wc command will display the file name along with the count of lines, words and characters stored in it. Using | (pipe symbol) at the terminal, will create a pipeline to connect two commands as follows:

$ls | wc

This command will simply connect the output of ls command to the input of wc command.

www.ingramcontent.com/pod-product-compliance
Ingram Content Group UK Ltd.
Pitfield, Milton Keynes, MK11 3LW, UK
UKHW021926190726
13853UKWH00002B/871

9 798888 334768